crabbing

Also by Alison Hackett

The Visual Time Traveller: 500 Years of History, Art and Science in 100 Unique Designs

crabbing

alison hackett

21C
RENAISSANCE

Published in April 2017 by 21st Century Renaissance, Fumbally Exchange, 5 Dame Lane, Dublin D02 HC67

www.21cr.ie

First edition

Copyright © Alison Hackett 2017

The moral right of the author, Alison Hackett, has been asserted. No part of this publication may be reproduced in any form or by any means without the prior permission of the publisher

British Library Cataloguing in Publication Data
A catalogue record for this book is available on request from the British Library

ISBN 978-0-9927368-2-8 (paper)

The text of this book is composed in Baskerville with the cover title in Tschischold

Layout by 21st Century Renaissance
Cover illustration & design by Nick Geoghegan

Printed in Ireland by Dundalgan Press (W. Tempest Ltd.)

Acknowledgments

The open access Dublin Writers' Forum led by the poets Anne Tannam and Fióna Bolger, has played no small part in helping this writer grow wings. Their critiquing method is essential, fresh and non-judgmental. I am especially grateful to Anne for her help in editing *Crabbing*. Her wisdom and advice was invaluable - when to shorten, what to leave out, how to sift the past from the present - making it possible for me to let go and press the print button.

The poem *But it never was to be* includes the first stanza of *They told me, Heraclitus, they told me you were dead*, a translation by William Johnson Cory (1823-1892) of the epitaph Callimachus wrote for his friend Heraclitus, who died c.a.260BC.

My thanks to the Dalkey Writers' Workshop which I attended a number of times. They were the first to hear and respond positively to *I am Éire*. The *Irish Examiner* published a version of this poem, as a letter to the editor, in 2016.

For his encouragement and practical advice I thank Gerard Smyth, poetry editor of *The Irish Times*, who led a workshop I attended at the Cork International Poetry Festival in 2016.

For showing me how to turn an anger poem into a love poem (at the Doolin Writers' Weekend in March 2016) I am indebted to the poet Stephen Murray.

For travelling with me I thank Elisabeth Muller.

for my father, Ronnie
8 June 1924 – 17 September 2015

I guillotine the past
the past is guillotined

an origami crane
enfolded in itself

holding skin to skin
I don't know where
you end and I begin

Contents

Introduction	xii
I	
Time is elastic	1
Currabinny	2
Shorn	4
Homeward bound	6
Rocky Bay	7
Salty tears	8
Gone	9
Alone	9
Where you lie	10
Awake at 5am	12
I met you on the Dart today	14
Coomakista	15
Cold day	16
II	
Hot day	20
Crabbing	23
Fisherman's friend	26
Echoing	27

But it never was to be	28
Panka's bible	29
37 South Mall	30
Two doves	32

III

The jeweller on the Grand Parade	37
Dún Laoghaire	39
I am Éire	42
Wolf child	44
Aisling	46
Blessé	49

p.s.

Poets and their editors down in the school yard	52

Introduction

The poem titled *Shorn* in this volume was first drafted in December 2012 not long after I had found my mother's unmarked grave - the place where I believed it to be. Several years later I discovered her resting place was on the other side of the graveyard, when my father was buried in the same plot. The poem *Where you lie* was written before I had realized the mistake.

Forty years earlier I was in boarding school when I was told that my mother, Lesley, had died. Not having known that she was dying the shock was profound and can never be separated from the fact that it was also my twelfth birthday that day. I had had the guilty pleasure that morning of enjoying the envy of the other boarders as they watched so many parcels (in the post) being passed down to me at breakfast. When I was called in from hockey for the fateful news, I ran in fast thinking that perhaps another present had arrived.

Being the youngest in the family it was all too easy to shield me from the truth that our mother had been fatally ill. The fall out in our family was immense with no road map for grief in those days. All my fear, abandonment and loss was pushed down deep. A knowledge that terrible things can happen must have marked me out as a quiet and serious child on my return to school.

In the following years, as a teenager, it was Mathematics that lured me into its embrace – a world of logic, elegance, pattern and proof.

Here I was safe. This I could control.

Once the grief started to spill over (as the fortieth anniversary of her death approached, a time when I was immersed in writing *The Visual Time Traveller*) it became a deluge, a post traumatic time. Nobody knew what was happening, least of all myself.

Writing poetry became one of the ways out of the rabbit hole in which I had been for so long. In carving words I found a way to express my truth: the voice of my twelve-year-old self emerging through the lens of a fifty-two-year-old reality.

They say publishing a poem is giving it a good burial. Off you go *Crabbing*. Out to sea for your Viking funeral. May you burn bright.

I

Time is elastic

Time is elastic
dust settles deep
but now and then
it stirs to life and
hurts beneath my skin

an ache
of a first born pain
rippling on
and on and on.

Currabinny

An old terrace at the end
of a cul-de-sac
looks out over a grassy bank
toward the harbour mouth.

The road there
winds past a boggy marsh
where once upon a time
we collected frogspawn.
Driving up the hill,
cloaked in darkness
by overhanging trees,
I pass the entrance
to Dring's farm,
the thatched cottage on the corner,
bungalows on the Green,
and slow to a crawl
to take the s-bend
make the last descent.

The estuary flickers through trees
Douglas firs climb steeply

up the left bank.
Past the Ferry House
the slip
Patterson's shed
a dry stone wall
a stony grey beach.

Quiet wooden pier
harbour opening out
the tide is in
I'm home.

Shorn

5th February 1973

Out playing hockey
in the afternoon
wind cuts through
my skinny frame.

Running racing
thwocking the ball
when out of nowhere
I am told to go
and see the principal.

I leave the game
as whistle shrieks.
Thud of goal is scored.

Running, I'm running in.

Knock on the door.
Into her office.
Dark. Sober. Serious.

High ceiling.
My sister there.

Why is she there too?

Your mother is gone
your mother is dead
the principal says
gently her fingers
stroke my knee.

Oh no.

No. No. No.

Not her. Not me.

Homeward bound

Our father's friend
drives us to the train.
He's wearing leather
driving gloves
of soft tan brown
with a button on the back.
So exotic, I'm fixated.
They seem to be seducing me.

We four play a game of cards
eyes sliding off each other
nothing much to say.
My reflection
shimmers in suspension
in the moving dark outside.
He meets us at the station.
Wild hair. A wildness in his eyes.

Rocky Bay

During the funeral
her mother's friend
brings her to walk the beach
at Rocky Bay.

A mean grey sky pressing down
gulls wheel and shriek in the cold wind.
A tidal drag sucking rivulets from the sand.

In the evening the fire is lit, curtains drawn
the hum and murmur of the crowd
chicken fricassée and rice is served.
It smells like a party.

Salty tears

Salty tears

cascade down

over gravel

across grass

melting stones

descend into the sea.

Gone

She disappeared
left without a trace
said no words
made no last embrace
Was she ever really there?

Alone

I walk a lonely road
the road to nowhere
a nowhere place
that circles back inside
the circles of my head.

Where you lie

12/12/12

We find the grassy square
between some yawning stones
inscribed with other names.
A leafless tree stands sentry
at the corner of your plot,
roots reaching down
beneath a lacy shadow
cast across the green.
We used a hand-drawn map
to find the grave.
He'd been the day before.

The estuary view
has long since gone
since built up houses
block the way, but the
curlew's cry can still be heard,
is what he wrote to say.

We leave some shells

beneath the tree,

small tokens of

our knotted loss.

Forty years unfurl.

Unspent grief erupts in me.

Awake at 5am

Awake at 5am
in tears
an overwhelming urge
to cradle you
so gently back
into your grave
your grave is warm
inside my mind
I won't let you be
too cold in there
but better still
come back to me
so I can breathe
one final touch
and whisper
of hello.
I open out
to embrace you
but arms collapse
around my self

an aching absent space

I want to lie

beside your bones

as near to you as me.

I met you on the Dart today

About the same age

as you would be now.

Tall and elegant

in a jaunty French beret

and coat of softest wool,

long and grey and chic.

I asked where it was bought

it had to be designer?

Italy, of course was the simple answer.

You'd been to Malahide

to see your younger sister,

your blood line of connection

an anchor in your life.

You'd lost your man some years ago

and moved to somewhere safe,

with fourteen grandchildren,

three adoring sons, and a daughter to adore.

I met you on the Dart today.

Coomakista

Last night I drove by Coomakista
to feel your presence in the air.

An old tree in the garden
holding inner rings of time,
sapling memory snug inside
its toughened bark.

I miss your love
the curls of you in me.

Cold day

on mountain walk
in snow
the sharpest
feel of air
family scattered wide
but you stay near
our belly chord
connecting us
connected in my mind

making snowballs
hands began to chill
and turn to pain
I turn to you for help
and in the kindest kind of way
you lift your jumper up
so frozen hands
on belly warm
can tingle back to life

I know it must

be hurting you

to feel my frosty hands

but I also know

that mother love

will always let

her child hurt back

in slightly

stinging ways

II

Hot day

sun beats down
baking hot
the woollen rug

beneath my skin
my boyish frame
lies prone

I'm profiled
in the elbowed
angles of my arms
.
flicker of cool
grass between my toes
just reaching out

and over tartan fringe
my sister starts
to write a word

with gentle finger
oh so slowly

on my back

the feeling is delicious
my sensate brain is
languid half awake

then the cognate
part kicks in with
wheels and cogs

that twist and turn
to deconstruct
the mystery word

gravel darkens
as sun slants
a slab of shade

toward the sea
cool air glances
off my reddened skin

these smarting legs

a burning proof

of sun that's trapped within

Crabbing

We head out in the clinker built punt,
salt and dirt and streaks of rotten wood
trapped in its layers of varnish.
The seagull engine putters out its beat -
a staccato morse code message
of our journey out to sea.

It takes an hour to make it
round the headland.
Open sea stretching down -
Spain, Africa, Antarctica beyond.
We hug the coast to find the way,
to find the place we know, Ringabella bay.

A swell surges us onto a sea
of thick ribbony weed
breaking through the surface in a mass
of loops and strips and arcs
of glistening brown, a life-like feeling
to its heaving rhythm with the waves.

We clamber out on barnacle
encrusted rocks and lodge an anchor
in the crevice of a channel
grooved into the rock;
the boat now safely linked by metal chain,
from sea to land, and land to sea.

In ancient holes we search for crabs
that ever will return. A bladdered frond
of seaweed swept aside, wafts its slow way back,
but not before a rusted red-brown crab
through watery lens is seen. A male.
Great black pincer folded in along its shell.

With iron hook I try to snag him under claw.
Fierce rattle of retreat and battle in the hole
until I feel his grip, and slowly haul him out,
shell scraping on the jagged rock.
"A big one. Watch out!
Could break your thumb." My father says.

Now the female. Deeper in the hole,
(the male no longer guarding her).
Smaller, plumper, sweeter flesh inside.
My hook scrapes the edges
of a vacant rocky place. No soft shell she,
no hard shell her. She's gone.

Homeward bound we pass the lighthouse,
Weavers Point, the Perch, the Can.
Twelve crabs piled on a seaweed bed,
strewn across the bottom of the boat.
They froth and bubble in the choking air,
a soft sight amongst their powerful claws.

Fisherman's friend

We drive to Carrigaline,
pretending I am small
when suddenly he pulls in
to take a Fisherman's Friend,
a sweet to keep him breathing
through the five miles ahead.

"I feel great when I'm driving"
he says, pulling back onto the road.

Echoing

The nurse and I pull the cover
over his frail and bony legs.
"You are like two angels." He says.

Later he tells me about the time
his father and aunt, Maud, went
to give morphine to their brother Wilkie,
dying in the wooden house he'd built
on Spanish island; and how she heard him
calling for her during the night. "Maud. Maud."

He's crying telling me this
the catch in his voice
echoing that other loss we share.
"I'm alright. I'm alright now." He says.

But it never was to be

He asked for a wicker coffin
his feet toward the sea
noted who to say the Eulogy
what the Epitaph might be.

He wanted to read a poem
at the funeral of his friend:

They told me, Heraclitus, they told me you were dead,
They brought me bitter news to hear and bitter tears to shed.
I wept as I remembered how often you and I
Had tired the sun with talking and sent him down the sky.

Panka's bible

In the bible by his bed
I find a cutting of a poem
with the opening line
The darkness of my grief is over

His grandfather, Panka,
first held it in his hands
a page mottled by time
inscribed in fountain pen:

Richard Belton
With his mother's love
17th August 1872

37 South Mall

The marble fireplaces
had been ripped out,
rubble spewing
into the Georgian room,
the Waiting Room,
a war zone.

Some fragments
remained. Reminders.
A handwritten price list,
for fillings and tooth removals,
stuck at an awkward angle on the door.
An old green jacket and tartan cap
hanging on the cast iron coat-stand.
Why, I wondered.
"So it looks like someone's here."

A dirty outline on the wall
where the roll-topped desk
used to be, mahogany curves
holding testament,
eloquent letters composed

in ink, kindly requesting
the bill to be settled,
when convenient.

The workroom out back
coated in a film of white dust.
I think of his patients
biting down
on the soft warm wax
leaving an impression
of teeth, and later,
when it had cooled,
him, pouring in
plaster of Paris,
to make a rigid cast.

Hundreds of them
lying there, cast aside.

In the attic
rain plinks into metal cans.
Above, a ragged scar of open sky.

Two doves

Two doves
on the tree
this morning.
A white birch
with peeling bark
and yellowed
trembling leaves
still clinging
to a former life.

Their backs to me
they canoodle
once or twice
heads entwined
in curved embrace.
Grey feathers
softly pillow him to her
a side by side refrain
an old and faithful touch.

A flash of fan-tails
tipped in white

as nature calls them

back to flight.

III

The jeweller on the Grand Parade

They announced his death in the paper.
He'd run off with an opera singer
leaving her with eleven children
running riot in the big house
with the pampas grass in front.

Word was he'd
gone to South America,
like Fitzcarraldo in the jungle,
dreaming of an opera house
he'd build in Iquitos.

A century later I find him
glowing on my screen
in faded script transformed,
my great grandfather,
Edward Hawksworth Hackett

no birth date, parents,
siblings, uncles, aunts,
his lineage eluding -

a threadbare place
in the weave of me.

When her mother arrived to help
she found them roller skating
on the table in the dining room
marks etched in mahogany.

Dún Laoghaire

A chunk of steel-blue sea under endless blue sky is framed by the off-white terraces lining Mellifont Avenue; it draws me down, down to the sea in this town of kings, Kingstown, Dún Laoghaire. The east and west piers reach out in a wide embrace, granite arms of a sleeping giant. Over the pier walls Howth hill beckons ending the wide sweeping curve of Dublin bay. Looking back inland the Sugar Loaf, a clear outline, a mini Vesuvius, amidst the undulating hills. Victorian terraces, port structures and a triple of spires – the Mariner's church, St Michael's tower that survived the 1896 fire and the Town Hall clock - jostling for position along the seafront. Open space and urban life in peaceful juxtaposition.

Terrace living for hundreds, an exercise in tolerance. Dog barking, baby mewling, piano tinkling, hammer thumping – no matter, live and let live. The daily "Hi", "How are you?", "Grand", "Weather's good", oiling a community spirit not often articulated yet mostly felt; the liberal left-leaning politics of the town emerging when the nation votes: Dún Laoghaire bucking the trend or leading the way, depending on how you look at it. Ann in the flower shop; John in the corner shop with a world wide web of newspapers yellowing in the breeze outside – Le Monde and Die Zeit sitting cheek by jowl with the Longford Leader and the Anglo Celt.

I walk the pier in all weathers, once packed with snow right to the end. The icy wind and white cloaked stone set against near-black sea sears a flash of the Baltics onto my brain. St Petersburg for a moment? Six months later a hot summers day, warm honey coloured granite and a salty wind whipping the yachts' wires clanking against their masts and suddenly I am on a Greek island. Was this what Joyce was thinking over a century ago when he looked out from the Martello tower, glimpsed just along the coast? Was it then that Leopold Bloom was born, destined to spend the 16th of June wandering Dublin in an echo of Odysseus's epic journey on the Ionian sea?

It's a clear night and once again I walk toward the sea, the pier, my homing point. I tread softly on the footsteps of thousands before me. The lights on Howth hill wink from across the darkness of the bay. Near, yet far. The sea is in my bones, my bones won't last too long inland.

Cities on the sea – San Francisco, San Sebastián, Boston, Barcelona, Nice and Naples – they all whisper to me in Dún Laoghaire.

I am Éire

I am Éire
        high on
                    the gas of 1916
        floating on
the cloud
        of a Clontarf dream

I am Éire
word-fire flickering in
the belly of my soldier messenger
but little does he know
of the forked tongues
of dealers in the body politic

I am the free state
part-whole
whole-part
my phantom limb in pain
an inconvenient spot on my
self-determined gain

I am the North
the Northern Ireland fix
part longing to belong
but my south
my east my west
a Britannia-Éire mix

I am Ireland
a land
a dream
a grá
a place you can call home
no matter where you are.

Wolf child

In the woods of Lower Saxony
near Helpensen
he is found in 1724.
Feral, grunting,
running on all fours.
He knows not how to cry.
They call him Peter the Wild Boy.

Eyes wary,
alert, ready to flee
at the slightest sound,
he fears the touch
of human hands.
They wonder if he is of God.

In a forest of Songy
in Champagne
she is found in 1731.
Half-child half-wolf
running on all fours
she hasn't learned to cry.
They call her the Maid of Châlons

Eyes wary,

alert, ready to flee

at the slightest sound.

She begins to love

their touching human hands.

They wonder if she knows of God.

Aisling

A mewling babe
I breathe you in
I drink your scent
no boundary
yet between us
though the
formal chord
was cut.

Is it you crying
on this dewy
winter morn?
Or is it me?
It feels the same.

Our separation
not to come
until at
two years old
you start
to play a game
of swapping roles

instructing me
to be the girl.

Down I sit
on child sized
chair at child
sized table.

"Girl" you say
"Drink your tea."
"Yes Mum."
I acquiesce
and wonder at
that well
worn path
to an
existential I.

Our two
connected lives
a narrative
an arc

an analogue
of time.

Blessé
for Justin

You inflict wounds with no malign intent
just careful cuts to take malign parts out.
Your hands are gentle, even cutting food.
Once in a restaurant you said you couldn't
be eating body parts you recognized,
and, by the way, that looks like
a rabbit's aorta to me.

That time we found a bird with a broken wing
in the yard, trembling,
one wing hopelessly flapping,
trying to lift itself to flight.
You took a stone to end its life.
I couldn't look. I wanted the miracle
of a wing repaired or time turned back.

p.s.

Poets and their editors down in the school yard

Miss! Miss! Jack just puked
up his last three stanzas,
Simon's after standing in it.

For God's sake
I'm a professional
do I have to deal with this?
Word vomit stinks like hell.
Get Beckett from
the janitor's room.
He can clean it up.
No ifs, ands or buts
(and tell him to bring the bleach).

Now. Where was I?
Oh yes. Sally.
In my opinion
her assonance is more like
cognitive dissonance.
Give her an enema

for her vowel problem,
and tell her to stick to a diet
of consonants
and glottal stops.

Got to run.
Meeting Larkin.
Parents complaining
their darling little darlings
won't take out
any fucking words.

Gardening leave.
Don't give me that look -
can't he write nature poems?

THE VISUAL TIME TRAVELLER
500 Years of History, Art and Science in 100 Unique Designs

Cast your mind back to the first decade of the 16th Century. What is happening? Leonardo da Vinci is painting the *Mona Lisa* and Michelangelo chips away at his sculpture of *David* while, in Rome, a lunar eclipse is observed by Copernicus. On the southern Atlantic Ocean a Portuguese explorer, João da Nova, discovers the island of St Helena – the place where Napoleon will be exiled over two hundred years later.

Now visit the years between 1895 and 1900 and here find Bram Stoker busy writing *Dracula* while blood-thinning Aspirin is being invented. X-rays are discovered, *The Importance of Being Ernest* by Oscar Wilde is first performed and Cézanne realizes the possibilities of modern art in his painting, *The Bathers*.

Re-ignite your inner curiosity with this graphically curated journey through history, art and science since the Renaissance. Dip inside and take off on your own historical journey. Browse with your intellect and fly with your imagination.

Alison Hackett was born in Cork and educated at Glengara Park School and Trinity College Dublin from which she graduated in Mathematics and Economics in 1982. She is the founder of 21st Century Renaissance, a movement dedicated to using original design combined with writing to influence change and raise debate across a wide section of society. Her belief is that an educational system must enable young people to become compassionate clear imaginative thinkers and life-long learners.

She worked as the Institute of Physics representative in Ireland for almost thirteen years. During that time she conceived of the idea for *The Visual Time Traveller* (2013) which was selected by an international jury as a finalist in the Global Irish Design Challenge of 2015.

She lives in Dún Laoghaire close to the sea, but not quite as close as her first home in Currabinny on the south coast of Ireland.